What Passes Here
for Mountains

Books by Matt Morton

Improvisation Without Accompaniment
What Passes Here for Mountains

What Passes Here for Mountains

Matt Morton

The Cox Family Poetry Chapbook Series

Carnegie Mellon University Press
Pittsburgh 2022

Acknowledgments

Grateful acknowledgments to the editors of the journals in which the following poems first appeared:

AGNI: "Westerly," "After the Festival"
The Hopkins Review: "The Stacks," "The New Science"
The Missouri Review: "Early Sunday Morning"
Los Angeles Review of Books: "From West Texas"
Subtropics: "Rare Snow in Rome"
Washington Square: "Exit Strategy"

What Passes Here for Mountains by Matt Morton is the second volume in The Cox Family Poetry Chapbook Series of Carnegie Mellon University Press. The Press administrators and staff express their profound appreciation to Courtney, Lisa, and Jordan Cox for their generous support.

Cover art by Susan Cantrick, *sbc159*, acrylic on linen, 55x46 cm, 2013.

Book design by Connie Amoroso

Library of Congress Cataloging-in-Publication Data

Names: Morton, Matt, 1987- author.
Title: *What passes here for mountains* / Matt Morton.
Description: First. | Pittsburgh : Carnegie Mellon University Press, 2022. | Series:
  The Cox family poetry chapbook series | Summary: "Matt Morton's What Passes
  Here for Mountains presents a mind caught in the grips of spiritual crisis. These
  poems take the reader on a journey across locales ranging from the West Texas des-
  ert to the bustling streets of Rome, from the social realm of festivity and ritual to
  the privacy of the imagination. Along the way, the search for meaning and stability
  within a world in constant flux is enlivened by a surrealist vitality. Cézanne and
  Shakespeare's Caliban commingle with indie rock musicians and Humpty Dumpty.
  A mystical encounter with an Edward Hopper painting meets the mundanity of
  waking again to one's morning routine. Poems of wry self-deprecation are juxta-
  posed with quiet meditations on memory, grief, and the relationship between the
  self and the cosmos" —Provided by publisher.
Identifiers: LCCN 2021044908 | ISBN 9780887486777 (trade paperback)
Subjects: LCGFT: Poetry.
Classification: LCC PS3613.O77867 W48 2022 | DDC 811/.6--dc23
LC record available at https://lccn.loc.gov/2021044908

for Corey Marks

Contents

Westerly

Like a Montana freeway, that arrow
of cloud once urged us on toward the sea. Big Sky
Country, Swan Lake Wilderness—this

was back in the heyday of pre-post-punk,
of Pioneer Romanticism, before the names all
huddled together and conspired to get weird

on us, sprouted their bulbous tails. And decades
prior, you could even break bread with a man
like Cézanne, he who happened to glimpse

fortuitously the mountain, his "beau motif,"
through a budget train-car window smudged
with children's fingerprints, as he stormed

through France. But the epidemic spreads.
The neighborhood Flower Spot
is on its last legs. If you'd like, you can contribute

to the indigo zeitgeist at Stefan's Magic
Biergarten, on the patio which teems
with hand-me-down couches and flannelled

patrons shivering under the waxing moon.
Me? I am as the proverbial hitchhiker
on peyote, a method actor holed up

in his camo bivouac in the haunted woods,
awaiting further instructions. When I dream
I dream of a snowy owl which somehow

penetrates the barracks wall—I can't explain why
I wake each time in the tub, with shame. I left home
with an offering of resolving major chords,

but alas, they must be saved for another season,
for autumn is truant again and dueling
hurricanes are thumping the Gulf, revising the maps.

I secretly fear we have overlooked the essential.
Outside, humidity chokes the one-way streets.
This place is a prison, and dear to me.

From West Texas

The javelina crossed the interstate soundtracked by Satie's
"Gnossienne no. 2."

"To the northwest of us is a firing range, do not be alarmed at the
sounds of."

There was no trail. A tiny family on the summit.

Oil derricks pecking rhythmically at the earth on this our day of
thanks.

I wear a pair of old brown boots and my father's jacket.

The population of Alpine dips below 6,000 in accordance with the
season.

Suspicion that this world is a collection of seemings, a mixed bag.

My hand reaches for hers in the rented dark.

See the impression of the wind on sagebrush?

Fields of bunchgrass, hoofprints like crescent moons in the sand.

As context shifts so too identity, as in the case of a windmill placed
on the bottom of the ocean.

Yucca, juniper, caliche. Like a prepared Turner canvas, the pastel
bands of sky.

So tentative each carefully weighted step from stone to stone.

"The source of the ghost lights remains unknown to this day."

Inside the bookshop a girl describes a kestrel, her voice is a wind
chime.

Belief I conceal from most people I love that the absence of form
will assume a shape.

There are two churches in town and three service stations.

After sundown even the Milky Way must work up the courage.

Election signs wait at the edge of private property.

In his later work, the foreground figures merge with the
atmosphere.

What passes here for mountains.

For three years, this famine of the spirit.

When I run out of medicine my experience of the desert sharpens,
but I become lost in it.

The Middle Years

approach with enviable patience:
          a canoe-fleet poking deliberately
                    through midnight mist,
          trailing gentle fissures, fluid fault lines
time sews up. "Yes, the route

has been patchy at best, blemished
          with boring stretches past outlet malls,
                    cattle ranches, and the irritation
          at no real mountains to speak of,
no squalls to outpace, but soon

we will reach the steppes and
          then you will see what progress . . ."
                    The impression the earlier victories left
          has faded,
the sidewalk-chalk advertisements

rained away, and habitually
          the once cordial neighbors
                    avoid eye contact, dart
          like clown fish behind tapped aquarium glass.
I think I was there with you once.

I shy from considering those twin imposters
          flexing inside our traits,
                    throwing our voices beneath the dome
          in front of the artificial moat of penguins.
Or remembering a previous version

of you post-supper, recounting how "we woke
        in the valley's upper reaches, secured
                our gear and bouldered through Charon's
        Garden in footwear boasting
aggressive tread which is better

for sticking." On the drive home,
        on the charcoal thigh of my hiking pants
                your hand almost belonged,
        our progress suddenly stalled by
a longhorn steer as *high as*

a church we saw through separate windshields,
        respective vantages varying only just so,
                and yet. And summer, too, dwindles,
        though someone like me will probably go on
swearing "the downpour slicked the lime-

stone jungle gym, peppered
        with tiny arrows the natural spring
                where beneath our common gaze
        two cottonmouths lolled
on the mudbank." I have an inkling

I don't trust: the performance will persist
        so long as we model good behavior,
                excuse ourselves and others, patrol
        nightly the shadowy facades and leaf-
strewn avenues, nevertheless

perplexed when we come up
        for air, "but wasn't it the Patersons' maple
                that oranged overnight and proceeded
        to freeze for the rest
of the season?" Still, I have reason to worry

we have strayed from the program
        again. *My dear, I'd have walked you to the edge of
                the water,* which even now—right now—
        is darkly purling in this direction
beyond the wall of cattail spikes. Yes,

we rehearsed the stoic
        expressions for years in advance
                of their entrance, our practice
        a kind of *rebellion, which unhesitatingly gives
the strength of its love.* But to discover

one can't share anything—

Rare Snow in Rome

Everything only connected by "and" and "and."

And hearses whirlpooling around the equine statue.
And windswept, seasonal fires supplanting
controlled burns. And rumors of Kodiak bears
ransacking the shuttered library branch. And the collared
golfer bemoaning his slice into trees. And the girl
who watches her uncle slap the face of a cousin who pilfered
a piece of cake. And the monument's patina.
And the steelworkers on strike. And the bolded
above-the-fold last words of the larcenist, shot
by a cop in a parking garage: "I don't want to die,
I don't want to die." And the careful bowknots,
the silver lures, fake flies. And the sea stacks
looming through fog at Rialto Beach. And the prince
who considers excuses to skip the banquet,
to trash the bouquet. And the Gulf towns
evacuated in hurricane season, the anonymous streets
of debris. And the headless, winged statue
no longer adorning the prow of a ship—a period piece
from an era in which each hour still boasted
its own, particular texture. When, on the cutting-room floor,
you could still connect the scenes, *serious, engravable*, and trust
they would stay, like those impossible ice forts
the schoolchildren built yesterday
in the Eternal City, barely believing
their luck as they prepared to wage merry war
in pom-pom hats, darting in
and out of the lazy shadows cast by the grand basilica.

Baggage Claim

Ever rehearse your therapy sessions?
Me neither. Never have I woken glistening
and greeted my night sweats with glee.
Never fist-pumped at the sight
of a parking ticket or bothered
to trace my stock back to its roots,
that's how little faith I have
in those roots, although at least one died
atop the Alamo wall, wearing a brave face.
Legend has it he drew a line in the sand.
Turns out I'm a little teapot complete
with a tempest or six inside. *The clouds
methought would open and show riches
ready to drop upon me* but never
have I glimpsed beyond the shadow
of a shadow of a doubt the face of God
although I've prayed. Consequently
never make it past 3:08 of the Shostakovich
Passacaglia without tears. Go ahead,
I'll wait. Gotten so used to waiting
an expert I have become in tentative expectancy.
Never yet had the desire to do it but
have slurped escargot with the zeal of an amateur.
Have been on the receiving end of precisely
the amount of love I suspect is required
to circumvent the crow's clutches
almost. Have watched three caskets disappear
but never can I shake this hunch
that somewhere there exists a secret
chiffonier, in which are stored the blueprints

of this place, i.e., our home. Or a concert hall
where we might hear the prelude
to our births, an explanation for how
and why the rules that we inherited led us here.
Have more than once myself been guilty
of bloodless performance. Of finding,
beneath the mask, another mask.
Funny how this charade of being
all Humpty-Dumpty-together-again
is often the only thing that stops
delphiniums from nosing through the cracks.

The Stacks

appear bigger here, this space
not quaint enough to qualify as "study"
nor possessing a library's
       solemn, spacious grandeur. Though the room is
nondescript, dark, window-
       less, it impresses
by its suggestion of diligence, austere

devotion to a program
one fashions—in the style of old masters—
using idiosyncratic
       devices, familiar capacities,
with which one has no choice
       but to reacquaint
oneself over morning coffee, egg whites, toast.

One may be forgiven if
their magisterial occupation—
dusty lamplit looming-over
       that serves both to inspire and stunt progress—
fosters some fearfulness
       in the novice heart.
Each creased spine evinces past disappointment,

the author's broken promise
to provide a comprehensive blueprint,
according to which the student
       might begin—finally, today—to shed
learning's light—guttering
       like breeze-disturbed wicks
of recently lit fragrant candles—upon

conundrums, paradoxes,
specious truth-claims lurking in crannies of
opinions—hidden spiral
            staircases of the mind. But books are just
tools. Alone, they're helpless
            to prescribe surefire
cures for confusions children inherited

or gave mistaken birth to—
traitorous offspring!—along the journey's
circuitous winding. Forging
            her way through cobwebbed mental maps, landscapes
of uncertain purpose
            and shaded alcoves,
the student is advised to form her own self-

estimation—to regard
cautiously the bolded names who profess
with pride belying carelessness,
            "I am sole possessor of what you seek"—
and incline the ear toward
            that interior dark
pizzicato, most faithful of instructors.

Early Sunday Morning

—after Edward Hopper

Immaculate, this morning scene of storefronts.
The green and red façade, the quiet street.

The sacred hour contains no witnesses—
no peddlers hawking trinkets, no noisy kids

with sidewalk chalk, no bored barber leaning
against his pole—except for you, the absent

viewer intruding on the emptiness.
You are here, the artist says, and you are not.

And isn't this what you have always wanted?
To wake alone and wander deserted streets,

free of the others, apart from even yourself,
because the self has gone? Impossible

scene, precisely rendered: the half-drawn
shutters, blue and yellow awnings, stub

of a hydrant's thin shadow—everything held
in perfect balance because it has been left

unblemished by the frenzy of stray dogs,
the ebbing whine of a passing ambulance,

because the horizontals seem to promise
to "extend well beyond the painting's purview."

What fortitude it must require to face
a dream of safety one cannot inhabit,

to see without blanking at the certain loss,
the only hint of which is the off-center

suggestion of a tower—hardly there
save for the way its dark asymmetry

tinges the hour—and the dawning sense
of a strange climate encroaching, filling up

the street across which no stray newsprint blows.

After the Festival

Everything has so little to do with me.
It has to do with exploding purple
lilies and chatty baristas, newborns
absorbing Chopin, students protesting
the war outside the courthouse
on the square. Sometimes I think I care
so little about it. I would rather show off
my self to myself, adorned in my gaudy cap
and gown, for I am a proud alumnus of
the School of Sophistication. How awful
it is to discover that you've been
spitting out the hours, racing yesterday-
you on the elliptical as you slowly
trend toward dust. Outside, the train
containers amble through the canyon.
Slow parade of big black pills.
It wasn't always this way. Once
it seemed there was a simple hypothesis
we could test, a color-penciled map
that led to a cliff-top bungalow over-
looking the fog, overlooking the sea.
That was before we discovered what
weird bodies these are—all flailing limbs
and shy smiles and unwanted hair and
when the air moves through our throats
like so, it is called singing. An aria, a dirge.
Is there even a charted course to abandon?
But how big and blue and permanent
the mountains seem to be, how inviting
their names . . . Night waves knocking

against the jetty, faint constellation
of hearts. We are faulty machinery.
We arrive in our packaging complete
with an expiration date. But I am here
for now, not seasick on this ugly olive couch—
part controlled detonation, part string
of lucky guesses—reciting
the monologue I know
I cannot help but hope
will last forever.

The New Science

For instance, how we tend to regard the earth
      as a living thing, instead of the mute assemblage of orchids
      and limestone it has thus far proven to be, ever since
we were children, since before we were given names.

And also our habit of apprehending the trees as figures
      of speech, fragments of an oration the planet delivers
      solely for our benefit—the dead leaves like echoes,
alone, but also somehow part of the green canopy

that once conjured them. As if an identity includes
      the epithets it drags like a kite through the clouds.
      Couldn't it be true, what the reservoir whispered to us
in the dream? Something about the illogic of sailboats,

a clue we could almost decipher, as if the words
      had been strained through a colander. Was it not a kind
      of love we felt for the water, fortified at the picnic table
although there was no picnic, watching the waves

break against the artificial beach? We rush to build nests
      in the niches hidden between the years, but part of me
      still feels I don't belong here among the forests of signs,
the squirrels foraging in advance of winter, which again

has cast us in its shadow play, despite our polite refusals.
      And now it is almost too late. And the harvest moon
      beckons to us like a long-lost friend who never meant
any harm, her face full of pallor and resignation.

Tabula Rasa

The curtains' blue translucence argues eight, maybe
later. Damp sheets upon reentry and vague anxiety
slash shame, source unknown. The last time you existed
in the conscious realm—sleepily poring over a translation
from the French—things seemed mostly okay, "all part
of a process," on-track toward the track's mysterious,
singular destination. Now the air is full of visual snow.
Conspiring courtyard maples take advantage of similarities

to prop up a pretense of kinship, a shared mapleness.
They beg some question but don't tell you what it is.
Even the day appears to evolve from the seed of itself
in search of a form. The sky tries on partial cloud cover
for size, the forecast predicts a wintry mix. Unclear how
to proceed. But consider again that heavy thought
you harbor and conceal—can you sense it lurking beyond
the periphery of your awareness? The best-case scenario
may necessitate some bucking up. The percolator kicks on.
No matter the Wi-Fi's contrary evidence, your experience
consists entirely right here: inherited defensive posture,

clenched jaw, tongue pressed to the mouth's roof and all
your projected hopes imbuing the off-white surface
of the rented room with a seemingly endless series of names.
Each breath is a kind of erasure: a fact of living. Sipping
from a holiday mug in your respective time zone, in expanding
space-fabric of nearly inconceivable origin, you have woken
again to inhabit the idea of yourself, your last chance
at this particular instant. And this one. Think about it.

Exit Strategy

Most things are easy to forget.
Everyone lives on a floating island.
The biographical includes what happens
in the mind. Don't use that shampoo.
In terms of lighting, the difference
between natural and fluorescent is substantial.
How many friends can you truly say you have?
The dramaturgy demands that we sit rigidly
in Adirondack chairs, holding our breaths
in hopes of a miracle.
Could you draw a composite sketch
of all your past and present selves, each one
vying for supremacy and terrified of turning
into a ghost? So much happening at once:
geese deviating from migration patterns,
siblings drafting false-alarm suicide notes
in invisible ink. Each January
all the gingerbread walls come tumbling down.
After the squall, a shimmer.
What's the bluest thing you've ever seen?
To exist at all can seem a terrible thing
but there are times when I get the sense
that someone just out of sight is tracing
sparkling infinity signs on the air with a Roman candle,
or plinking "Clair de Lune" on a distant shore.
As when I wept, watching the disaster flick—
a cliffside crashes into a fjord
and the father takes his daughter in his arms.
If that sounds corny, imagine you're the father.
Imagine a giant wave

storming through the valley toward you
and the ones you love, the water
curling up like a scorpion's tail.
Lightning strikes a radio tower,
red blinking on, blinking off.
Yes, our case is terminal but
maybe it's possible to learn how to leave.
Maybe there's a logging road winding up to higher ground.
Time enough for the mountain in the mind
to become a mountain.

Books in the Cox Family Poetry Chapbook Series

2021
Elegiac, Charles Seluzicki

2022
What Passes Here for Mountains, Matt Morton
This Long Winter, Joyce Sutphen